THE MAGNIFICENCE
OF MAN

and

TRUTH—AND MORE

THE MAGNIFICENCE OF MAN

and

TRUTH—AND MORE

Russell M. Nelson

CLASSIC TALK SERIES

Deseret Book Company
Salt Lake City, Utah

Reprinted with permission.

Library of Congress Catalog Card Number: 97-78187

ISBN 0-87579-985-X

Printed in the United States of America   72082-4585B

10   9   8   7   6   5   4   3   2

THE MAGNIFICENCE
OF MAN

I invite you to ponder things magnificent. The word *magnificent* is derived from two Latin roots. The prefix *magni-* comes from a term meaning "great," and the suffix comes from the Latin *facere,* meaning "to make" or "to do." A simple definition of *magnificent,* then, might be "great deed" or "greatly made."

Think of the most magnificent sight you have ever seen. It could be a meadow in springtime filled with beautiful wildflowers. Or perhaps you have been awestruck, as have I, at the magnificence of a single rose. I have come to appreciate the magnificence of an orange, with each droplet of juice packaged in an edible container, joined with many other packets, grouped in sections, and all neatly wrapped in a disposable, biodegradable peel.

Some would say the most magnificent sight they have ever beheld is looking heavenward on a summer night, seeing stars beyond number dotting the sky. Those who have traveled in orbit through space say that their view of planet earth was one of the most magnificent sights ever observed by man.

Some might choose the view of the Grand Canyon at sunrise; others, the beauty of a mountain lake, river, waterfall, or desert. Some might select a peacock with its tail in full fan, or a handsome horse. Others would nominate the beauty of butterfly wings, or a hummingbird seemingly suspended in midair while feeding. These magnificent sights are wondrous beyond measure. They are all "great deeds" of our divine Creator.

Now, ponder the magnificence of what you see when you look in the mirror. Ignore the freckles, the unruly hair, or the blemishes, and look beyond to see the real you—a child of God—created by him, in his image.

If we peek beyond what we see in the mirror and lift the lid on the treasure chest of the marvelous attributes of our bodies, we can discover, at least in part, the magnificence of man.

EMBRYONIC DEVELOPMENT

In the first compartment of the treasure chest, we might look at the magnificence of human creation itself.

We don't know precisely how two germ cells unite to become a human embryo, but we do know that both the female cell and the male cell contain all the new individual's hereditary material and information, stored in a space so small it cannot be seen by the naked eye. Twenty-three chromosomes from both the father and the mother unite in one new cell. These chromosomes contain thousands of genes. A marvelous process of genetic coding is established, by which all the basic human characteristics of the unborn person are determined. A new DNA complex is thus formed and a continuum of growth is instituted—which results in a new human being. Approximately twenty-two days after two germ cells unite, a little heart begins to beat. At twenty-six days blood begins to circulate. Cells multiply and divide, some becoming differentiated to become eyes that see. Some become ears that hear, while others are destined to become fingers.

SPECIFIC ORGANS

In our treasure chest of understanding, each jewel merits admiration, appreciation, and awe. The eyes with which we see are magnificent. No doubt you have stood before the mirror, as have I, watching pupils react to changes in the intensity of light—dilating to let more light in, constricting to reduce the light allowed to reach the eyes' sensitive retinas. A self-focusing lens is at the front of each eye. Nerves and muscles synchronize the function of two separate eyes to produce one three-dimensional image. Eyes are connected to the brain, ready to record sights seen. No cords, no batteries, no external connections are needed; our visual apparatus is marvelous—infinitely more priceless than any camera money can buy.

If we admire good stereophonic equipment for sensing sound, we can appreciate the magnificence of the human ear. Compacted into an area about the size of a marble is all the equipment needed to perceive sound. A tiny tympanic membrane serves as the diaphragm. Minute ossicles amplify the signal, which is then transmitted along nerve lines to the brain, which registers the result of hearing. This marvelous sound system is also connected to the recording instrument of the brain.

A large portion of my life's study and research has been focused on the jewel of the human heart—a pump so magnificent that its power is almost beyond our comprehension. To control the direction of flow of blood within it, there are four important valves, pliable as a parachute and delicate as a dainty silk scarf. They open and close over one hundred thousand times a day—over thirty-six million times a year. Yet, unless altered by disease, they are so rugged that they can stand this kind of wear seemingly indefinitely. No man-made material developed thus far can be flexed so frequently and for so long without breaking.

The amount of work the heart does is amazing. Each day it pumps enough fluid to fill a 2,000-gallon tank. The work it performs daily is equivalent to lifting a 150-pound man to the top of the Empire State Building, while consuming only about four watts of energy—less than that used by a small lightbulb in your home.

At the crest of the heart is an electrical generator that transmits energy down special lines, causing myriads of muscle fibers to beat in coordination and in rhythm. This synchrony would be the envy of any orchestra's conductor.

All this power is condensed in the human heart—only about the size of one's fist, yet energized from within by an endowment from on high.

One of the most wondrous of all jewels in this treasure chest is the human brain with its intricate combination of power cells and recording, memory, storage, and retrieval systems. The brain serves as headquarters for the personality and character of each human being. The capacity of the brain is seemingly infinite. Wise men can become even wiser as each experience builds upon previous experience. Indeed, continuing exercise of the intellect brings forth increased intellectual capacity.

Each time I marvel at a computer and admire the work it can do, I respect even more the mind of man, which developed the computer. The human brain is certainly a recording instrument that will participate in our judgment one day as we stand before the Lord. The Book of Mormon speaks of the "bright recollection" (see Alma 11:43) and "perfect remembrance" (see Alma 5:18) we will have then. Each one of us carries that recording instrument guarded within the vault of the human skull.

We could spend hours—even a lifetime—studying the incredible chemical capacity of the liver, the kidneys, and any or all of the endocrine and exocrine glands of the body. Each is a shimmering jewel, worthy of our study and our deepest gratitude.

CONCEPTUAL CONSIDERATIONS

Now let us turn our attention to jewels in another compartment in the treasure chest of understanding. Let us consider some concepts that go beyond that of individual organ systems.

The first concept I would mention is that of reserve, or backup. In the theater, major actors have understudies. In electrical instruments, backup in the event of a power failure may be provided by batteries. Think of the backup provided by a number of paired body organs such as the eyes, ears, lungs, adrenal glands, and kidneys. In the event of illness, injury, or loss of one of these organs, the other is there ready to keep our bodily functions intact. In the event of loss of sight or hearing altogether, other sensory powers become augmented in a miraculous manner.

Some backup systems are not so apparent. For

example, crucial single organs, like the brain, the heart, and the liver, are all nourished by two routes of circulation, which minimizes damage in the event of loss of blood flow through any single blood vessel.

Another dimension of backup is that of collateral pathways. For example, if our nasal passageways are obstructed by a stuffy nose, we may breathe through our mouths. Similarly, collateral pathways may grow in the event of obstruction or severance of blood vessels or nerves.

Consider another concept—the body's self-defense. As I watched some three-year-old children playing one day, I saw them lap water from the sidewalk after it had spilled through a neighbor's garden. The germs they ingested were incalculable in number, but not one of those children became ill. As soon as that germ-infested water reached their stomachs, hydrochloric acid went to work to purify the water and to protect those innocent children's lives.

Think of the protection provided by the skin. Could you make, or even conjure in your mind how to create, a cloak that would protect you and at the same time perceive and warn against injuries that excessive heat or cold might cause? The skin does that. It even gives signals which indicate that another part of the body is ailing. The skin can flush and sweat with fever. When one is frightened or ill, it pales. When one is embarrassed, it blushes. It is replete with nerve fibers that communicate and often limit possible harm through perception of pain.

Pain itself is part of the body's defense mechanism. For example, sensory areas of the mouth guard the delicate esophagus, which has very few nerve fibers. Like a sentinel, the mouth receives warnings that protect the tender esophagus from becoming burned from drinks that are too hot.

The body also produces chemical antibodies in response to infections. These antibodies not only combat infection; they also persist with memory to strengthen resistance in days to come. When military conscription was required in World War II, soldiers from isolated rural areas had much less immunity and were more prone to infections than were those from highly populated urban areas, whose resistance was better developed.

Closely related to the concept of self-defense is that of self-repair. Broken bones mend and become strong once again. If I were to break one of the legs of a chair, that leg would never heal itself. Yet many of us walk on legs that once were broken. Lacerations of the skin heal themselves. A leak in the circulation will seal itself. Circulatory systems outside the body do not have this power—something I gained appreciation for early in my research career when working to create an artificial heart-lung machine. Whenever tubing in the machine sprang a leak, it meant long hours cleaning up in the lab. Never did a leak in the machine seal itself.

The concept of self-renewal is remarkable. Each body cell is created and then regenerated from the earth's elements according to the "recipe" or formula contained within our unique genes. The average red blood corpuscle, for example, lives about 120 days. Then it dies and is replaced by another. Each time we bathe, thousands of dead and dying cells are scrubbed away and replaced by a younger crop. To my thinking, this process of self-renewal prefigures the process of resurrection.

Another remarkable concept is that of auto-regulation. In spite of wide fluctuations in the temperature of man's environment, the body's temperature is carefully controlled within certain narrow bounds.

Have you wondered why you can't swim under water very long. Auto-regulation limits the time you can hold your breath. As breath is held, carbon dioxide accumulates. Partial pressure of carbon dioxide is monitored continuously by two carotid bodies situated in the neck. They transmit signals through nerves to the brain, which then sends stimuli to muscles of respiration, causing them to work so that we might inhale a new refreshment of oxygen and eliminate the carbon dioxide.

The number of such systems exceeds our ability to enumerate them. Sodium, potassium, water, glucose, protein, and nitrogen are but a few of the many constituents continuously monitored by chemical regulators within our bodies.

Consider the concept of adaptation. People on the earth dwell amidst climatic and dietary differences of vast variety. Eskimos in the Arctic Circle consume a diet with a large component of fat, which is acceptable and even necessary to sustain life in a cold climate. Polynesians, on the other hand, eat a diet appropriate for a tropical environment. These different groups work and adapt to varying conditions and to the foods that are available where they live.

The concept of identity in reproduction is marvelous to contemplate. Each of us possesses seeds that carry our unique chromosomes and genes, which help determine specific cellular identity for our children. For this reason, tissues surgically transplanted from one person to another can only survive if the host's immune response, which clearly recognizes tissues foreign to one's own inherited genetic formula, is suppressed. Truly we are blessed with the power to have children born in the likeness of parents on earth as well as in heaven.

As we consider self-defense, self-repair, and self-renewal, an interesting paradox emerges.

Limitless life could result if these marvelous qualities of the body continued in perpetuity. If we could create anything that could defend itself, repair itself, and renew itself without limit, we could create perpetual life. That was what our Creator did with the bodies he created for Adam and Eve in the Garden of Eden. If they had eaten the fruit of the tree of life, they would have lived forever. According to the Lord as revealed through his prophets, the fall of Adam instituted the aging process, which ultimately results in physical death. We do not understand all the chemistry, but we are witnesses of the consequences of growing old. Those consequences assure us that there is a limit to the length of life upon the earth.

Of course, our bodies can develop troubles that do not repair themselves with time. Death, when it comes, may seem untimely to our mortal minds. But we need to have a larger view—

that death is part of life. Alma tells us that "it was not expedient that man should be reclaimed from this temporal death, for that would destroy the great plan of happiness" (Alma 42:8; see also D&C 29:32).

When severe illness or tragic injuries claim an individual in the prime of life, we can take comfort in this fact: The very laws which could not allow life to persist here are the same eternal laws that will be implemented at the time of the resurrection, when that body "shall be restored to [its] proper and perfect frame" (Alma 40:23).

Thoughts of life, death, and resurrection bring us to face crucial questions. How were we made? By whom? and Why?

CREATED BY GOD

Through the ages, some without scriptural understanding have tried to explain our existence by pretentious words such as *ex nihilo* (out of nothing). Others have deduced that, because of certain similarities between different forms of life, there has been a natural selection of the species, or organic evolution from one form to another. Many of these people have concluded that the universe began as a "big bang" that eventually resulted in the creation of our planet and life upon it.

To me, such theories are unbelievable! Could an explosion in a printing shop produce a dictionary? It is unthinkable! Even if it could be argued to be within a remote realm of possibility, such a dictionary could certainly not heal its own torn pages or renew its own worn out corners or reproduce its own subsequent editions!

We are children of God, created by him and formed in his image. Recently I studied the scriptures to find how many times they testify of the divine creation of man. Looking up references that referred to *create*, *form* (or their derivatives), with either *man*, *men*, *male*, or *female* in the same verse, I found that there are at least fifty-five verses of scripture that attest to our divine creation. I have selected one to represent all the verses that convey the same conclusion:

"The Gods took counsel among themselves and said: Let us go down and form man in our image, after our likeness; . . .

"So the Gods went down to organize man in their own image, in the image of the Gods to form they him, male and female to form they them" (Abraham 4:26–27).

SPIRITUAL DISCERNMENT

I believe all of those scriptures that pertain to the creation of man. But the decision to believe is a spiritual one, not made solely by an understanding of things physical, for we read that "the natural man receiveth not the things of the Spirit of God: for they are foolishness unto him: neither can he know them, because they are spiritually discerned" (1 Corinthians 2:14).

It is incumbent upon each informed and

spiritually attuned person to help overcome such foolishness of men who would deny divine creation or think that man simply evolved. By the Spirit, we perceive the truer and more believable wisdom of God.

With great conviction, I add my testimony to that of my fellow Apostle Paul, who said, "Know ye not that ye are the temple of God, and that the Spirit of God dwelleth in you?

"If any man defile the temple of God, him shall God destroy; for the temple of God is holy, which temple ye are" (1 Corinthians 3:16–17).

DUALITY OF MAN

The Lord said that "the spirit and the body are the soul of man" (D&C 88:15). Therefore, each one of us is a dual being—a biological (physical) entity, and an intellectual (spiritual) entity. In the beginning, man, the intellectual entity, was with God. Our intelligence "was not created or made," nor can it be (see D&C 93:29).

That spirit, joined with a physical body of such remarkable qualities, becomes a living soul of supernal worth. The psalmist so expressed this thought:

"When I consider thy heavens, the work of thy fingers, the moon and the stars, which thou hast ordained;

"What is man, that thou art mindful of him? . . .

"For thou hast made him a little lower than the angels, and hast crowned him with glory and honour" (Psalm 8:3–5).

Why were we created? Why are we here? Why are we upon the earth?

God has made it plain over and over again that the world was made for mankind. We are here to work out our divine destiny, according to an eternal plan that was presented to us in the great council of heaven. Our bodies have been created to accommodate our spirits, to allow us to experience the challenges of mortality and continue our eternal progression.

AVOID DESECRATION OF THE PHYSICAL TEMPLE

When we understand our nature and our purpose on earth, and that our bodies are physical temples of God, we will realize that it is sacrilege to let anything enter the body that might defile it. It is irreverent to let even the gaze of our precious eyesight or the sensors of our touch or hearing supply the brain with memories that are unclean or unworthy.

Could any of us lightly regard precious seeds of reproduction—specifically and uniquely ours—or disregard the moral laws of God, who gave divine rules concerning their sacred use?

We know we are children of God—that he created us and that he has given us agency to choose. We also know that we are accountable to him. He has defined the truth and prescribed commandments. Obedience to his law will bring us joy. Disobedience of those commandments is defined as sin. Because we live in a world that seems increasingly reluctant to designate dishonorable deeds as sinful, the scriptures warn us, "Fools make a mock at sin: but among the righteous there is favour" (Proverbs 14:9).

No one is perfect. Some may have sinned grievously in transgressing God's laws. But God is merciful. We can repent and learn to control our appetites of the flesh.

Substances such as alcohol, tobacco, and harmful drugs are forbidden by the Lord. We have similarly been warned about the evils of pornography and unclean thoughts. Appetites for these degrading forces can become addictive. In time, physical or mental addictions enslave *both* the body and the spirit. Full repentance from these shackles, or from any other yokes of sin, must be accomplished in this life, while we still have the aid of a mortal body to help us develop self-mastery.

When we truly know our divine nature, we will want to control our appetites. We will focus our eyes on sights, our ears on sounds, and our minds on thoughts that are a credit to our physical creation as a temple of our Father in Heaven. In daily prayer, we will gratefully acknowledge him as our Creator and thank him for the magnificence of our physical temple. We will heed his counsel.

MORE YET TO LEARN

Though we cannot fully comprehend the magnificence of man, when we understand more about our nature, we may join with Jacob in this marvelous declaration:

"Behold, great and marvelous are the works of the Lord. How unsearchable are the depths of the mysteries of him; and it is impossible that man should find out all his ways. . . .

"For behold, by the power of his word man came upon the face of the earth, which earth was created by the power of his word. . . .

"Wherefore, brethren, seek not to counsel the Lord, but to take counsel from his hand" (Jacob 4:8–10).

For years I have attended scientific meetings of learned societies. Thousands of medical scientists and practitioners from all over the world participate in such assemblies annually, to learn about the latest scientific discoveries and procedures in the field of medicine.

The quest for knowledge is endless. It seems that the more we know, the more there is yet to learn. It is impossible that man may learn all the ways of God. But if we are faithful and are deeply rooted in the scriptural accounts of God's magnificent creations, we will be better able to understand future scientific discoveries. All truth is compatible because it all emanates from God.

BEWARE OF FALSE DOCTRINE

Of course, we know that "there is an opposition in all things" (2 Nephi 2:11). In the world, even many so-called "educators" teach ideas that are contrary to divine truth. We must be mindful of this prophetic counsel:

"O the vainness, and the frailties, and the foolishness of men! When they are learned they think they are wise, and they hearken not unto the counsel of God, for they set it aside, supposing they know of themselves, wherefore, their wisdom is foolishness and it profiteth them not. And they shall perish.

"But to be learned is good if they hearken unto the counsels of God" (2 Nephi 9:28–29).

We need not be reminded that the work and glory of the Lord are opposed by the forces of Satan, the master of deceit. Remember, "Man may deceive his fellow-men, deception may follow deception, and the children of the wicked one may have power to seduce the foolish and untaught, till naught but fiction feeds the many, and the fruit of falsehood carries in its current the giddy to the grave" (JS–H 1:71, footnote).

Let us be wise and keep away from temptations and snares. Let us cautiously avoid "foolish and hurtful lusts, which drown men in destruction and perdition" (1 Timothy 6:9). Let us "flee these things; and follow after righteousness, godliness, faith, love, patience, meekness." Let us "fight the good fight of faith" and "lay hold on eternal life" (1 Timothy 6:11–12).

SPIRITUAL DOMINION

The magnificence of man is matchless. But, glorious as this physical tabernacle is, the body is designed to support something even *more* glorious—the eternal spirit, which dwells in each of our mortal frames. The great accomplishments of this life are rarely physical. Those attributes by which we shall be judged one day are spiritual. With the blessing of our bodies to assist us, we may develop spiritual qualities of honesty, integrity, compassion, and love. Only with the development of the spirit may we acquire "faith, virtue, knowledge, temperance, patience, brotherly kindness, godliness, charity, humility, [and] diligence" (D&C 4:6).

Let us pattern our lives after our great Exemplar, even Jesus the Christ, whose parting words among men included this eternal challenge: "What manner of men ought ye to be? . . . even as I am" (3 Nephi 27:27).

We are sons and daughters of God. He is our Father; we are his children. Our divine inheritance is the magnificence of man. I pray that we may honor and magnify it.

This is an edited version of a talk delivered at Brigham Young University on 29 March 1987 when Elder Nelson was serving as a member of the Quorum of the Twelve Apostles. The talk was published in the January 1988 edition of the *Ensign,* 64–69.

TRUTH—AND MORE

Those privileged to work in a university have a bond of brotherhood denoted by the very name "university." The first three letters, *uni,* imply "unity—to be one." The next syllable, *vers,* comes from the Latin word meaning "to turn."

All of us are literally "turned as one" toward a mutual goal, sharing a common commitment to truth, and to its omniscient Author. An international brotherhood binds scholars together even across political boundaries. Rising majestically above the babbling sea of European languages, one word has emerged unaltered as a symbol of that unity—*university.* At least in Latin, Danish, Dutch, English, French, German, Italian, Norwegian, Portuguese, Russian, Spanish, and Swedish, the stem of the word is the same. Only the grammatical ending differs among these languages.

From varying backgrounds and disciplines, we are joined in one common goal—to turn as one to the truth and to the other noble purposes for which a great university stands.

If my message deserves a title, I would choose "Truth—*and More,*" inviting you to consider the deficiency of the notion that simply knowing truth somehow frees us from any thoughtful consideration of its use and its power.

The mission of the university is indelibly intertwined with the glory of truth. Its researchers discover the truth, its teachers proclaim the truth, and its service to society applies the truth.

When I was in medical school, I was taught that one must never touch the human heart, for if one did, it would stop beating. That was the limit of our knowledge of the truth then. I remember our first experiments on animals during which we tenderly dared to incise the chest and open the pericardium (the sac around the heart) only after injecting novocaine to anesthetize the heart so it "might not know" we were coming. It worked. Subsequently, we found that the heart continued to function even if we didn't anesthetize it. It beat merrily on its way even if we touched it, held it, or stitched it. As a result of these more detailed experiments and the work of many researchers, all designed to find more of the truth, safe surgery on the heart has now become routine in most nations of the earth.

That background, drawn from my own personal experience, may serve to distinguish "relative" from "absolute" truth. In fact, early in my professional training, one instructor said that everything taught in medical school should have a sign posted on it: "This is our present understanding of the truth—until it is later shown to be false."

Of course, the truth isn't "relative." It is only man's understanding of the truth that is "relative."

Researchers realize that only a small sample of the totality of "absolute" truth is known. Therein lies the allurement of research. There are few rewards as exciting as the discovery of truth, through research well performed.

But truth proclaimed by Deity is as absolute as Deity, who defined such truth as "knowledge of things as they are, and as they were, and as they are to come" (D&C 93:24).

The glory of truth is revealed in these words of the Master: "If ye continue in my word, then are ye my disciples indeed; And ye shall know the truth, and the truth shall make you free" (John 8:31–32).

Truth literally makes us free from the bondage of ignorance.

Many great people have been imbued with a passion for truth. One of those was John Jaques, born in England 7 January 1827, a son of Wesleyan Methodist parents. In his youth, he recorded that he was earnestly seeking the true religion. After intensive study with LDS missionaries who taught him the gospel, he was baptized and became a member of The Church of Jesus Christ of Latter-day Saints in 1845 at age eighteen.

John's austere father, upset upon hearing this news, wrote: "I wished you . . . to attend the Wesleyan Chapel. They [the Mormons] do not teach you . . . to honor and obey your parents. I . . . hope you will give up the idea of belonging to such a party. . . . It is fiction."

John's reply, written 14 March 1847, when he was but twenty years of age, included these words:

"Dear Father, I would pray that I may be led and guided into all truth that I may understand the things of the Kingdom of God and carry my ideas to you . . . and be enabled to understand truth. . . .

"Before I conclude, I will . . . bear . . . humble testimony to the truth of the work which the Lord has commenced.

"Since I [joined the Church] my eyes have been opened and I have been able to understand the truth. I can bear testimony to the truth . . . of the doctrines . . . in The Church of Jesus Christ of Latter-day Saints."

John then likened the truth of the gospel to a diamond, while comparing "the low smattering of education of religionists" to "a rivulet's common pebble" (Stella Jaques Bell, *Life History and*

Writings of John Jaques, including a diary of the Martin Handcart Company, Rexburg, Idaho: Ricks College Press, 1978, 19–21).

At age twenty-three, John Jaques wrote these immortal lines:

Oh say, what is truth? 'Tis the fairest gem
That the riches of worlds can produce,
And priceless the value of truth will be when
The proud monarch's costliest diadem
Is counted but dross and refuse.

Yes, say, what is truth? 'Tis the brightest prize
To which mortals or Gods can aspire.
Go search in the depths where it glittering lies,
Or ascend in pursuit to the loftiest skies:
'Tis an aim for the noblest desire.

The scepter may fall from the despot's grasp
When with winds of stern justice he copes.
But the pillar of truth will endure to the last,
And its firm-rooted bulwarks outstand the rude blast
And the wreck of the fell tyrant's hopes.

Then say, what is truth? 'Tis the last and the first,
For the limits of time it steps o'er.
Tho the heavens depart and the earth's fountains burst,

Truth, the sum of existence, will weather the worst,
Eternal, unchanged, evermore.
(*Hymns*, 1985, no. 272.)

Brother Jaques spent his last years in the historian's office of the Church, where he labored as an assistant to the historian from 1889 until his death 1 June 1900.

It is of interest that earlier, as an elder, he became an active missionary affiliated with a branch at Stratford-upon-Avon, the home of William Shakespeare.

Speaking of the Bard, we recall the statement made through his character Polonius: "This above all: to thine own self be true" (*Hamlet*, Act 1, Sc. 3). Perhaps less well known are these lines spoken by Isabella in Act 5 of *Measure for Measure:*

This is all as true as it is strange:
Nay, it is ten times true; for truth is truth
To th'end of reck'ning.

That expression closely mirrors the teaching of the Lord: "Truth abideth and hath no end" (D&C 88:66).

The search for truth is not only institutional, it is individual. Thirty years ago, as we were embarking on an uncharted sea early in the development of human open-heart surgery, I scheduled only one such operation a month. Each operation was a skirmish with terror, usually bringing us face-to-face with death, with the unknown, and with limitations imposed by our own ignorance. That confrontation forced us to return to the laboratory to overcome the inadequacies encountered during the previous experience. Then, when fortified and prepared by solving a specific problem, we would enter again the whirlpool of another experience, learning little by little some of the truth upon which the principles of safe open-heart surgery one day could stand.

Truth was there all the time. It was absolute—part of the incontrovertibility of divine law that we had to know if we were to succeed. We moved toward that light a step at a time, gradually leaving in darkness the specters of fear, chance, and disaster.

My experiences as a surgeon taught me the remarkable potential for truth. It is a powerful sword—an instrument that can be wielded just like a surgeon's knife. It can be guided well to bless. But it can also be crudely applied to wound, to cripple, to damage, or even to destroy!

May I give you an illustration? Imagine a surgeon who has just operated upon a patient and found cancer invading vital organs of the body. It is widespread and beyond cure. With this knowledge, the surgeon approaches the family and the patient and coldly announces that the patient has advanced cancer, that he is beyond hope and is doomed to die. While discharging his duty to share that information, the surgeon has told the truth, but with utter abandon has then walked away from the turmoil that "truth" has left in its wake.

Another surgeon, with that same information and with compassion, approaches the family, speaks the truth, and then mercifully indicates that, even though the road ahead will be difficult and challenging, the patient and the family will not be forsaken. They will be supported with all the resources available to him as their caring physician.

Important as truth is, often we need truth *and more.*

Emily Dickinson expressed this concept poignantly: "The truth must dazzle gradually, or every man be blind" (*Poems of Emily Dickinson*, sel. Helen Plotz, New York: Thomas Y. Crowell Company, 14).

As a slogan that encourages truth *and more,* I like the four-way test of Rotary International:

1. Is it the truth?
2. Is it fair to all concerned?
3. Will it build goodwill and better friend-ships?
4. Will it be beneficial to all?

In holy writ, the word *truth* is coupled with the word *mercy* or its cognates forty-seven times. *Truth* is joined with forms of *right* or *righteousness* in forty-two passages of scripture.

The psalmist wrote, for example: "Mercy and truth are met together; righteousness and peace have kissed each other" (Psalm 85:10). This verse is then followed by the prophecy of the coming of the Book of Mormon: "Truth shall spring out of the earth; and righteousness shall look down from heaven" (Psalm 85:11).

A similar message comes from the Lord through the book of Moses: "Righteousness will

I send down out of heaven; and truth will I send forth out of the earth, to bear testimony of mine Only Begotten" (Moses 7:62).

We all might measure truth with the standard of mercy, if obedient to these passages from Proverbs: "Do they not err that devise evil? but mercy and truth shall be to them that devise good" (Proverbs 14:22). "By mercy and truth iniquity is purged" (Proverbs 16:6).

Those privileged to hold membership in the restored Church might well remember this psalm: "All the paths of the Lord are mercy and truth unto such as keep his covenant and his testimonies" (Psalm 25:10).

The psalmist added this observation: "But thou, O Lord, art a God full of compassion, and gracious, long-suffering, and plenteous in mercy and truth" (Psalm 86:15).

Otherwise, the sword of truth, cutting and sharp as a surgeon's scalpel, might not be governed by righteousness or by mercy, but might be misused carelessly to embarrass, debase, or deceive others.

I am reminded of a personal experience that you may find amusing. I was serving as a consultant to the United States government at its National Center for Disease Control in Atlanta, Georgia. Once while awaiting a taxi to take me to the airport after our meetings were over, I stretched out on the lawn to soak in a few welcome rays of sunshine before returning to the winter weather of Utah's January. Later I received a photograph in the mail taken by a photographer with a telephoto lens, capturing my moment of relaxation on the lawn. Under it was a caption, "Governmental consultant at the National Center." The picture was true, the caption was true, but the truth was used to promote a false impression. Yes, truth can even be used to convey a lie.

Indeed, in some instances, the merciful companion to truth is *silence*. Some truths are best left unsaid.

My mother expressed that thought to me often with this simple phrase, "Russell, if you can't say something nice about someone, say nothing." I might add, incidentally, that her injunction became a real challenge to me, as my entire professional life required my telling each patient about the abnormalities that he or she possessed.

We live in a day when politicians occasionally dig for "truth" that would degrade an opponent. We live in a time when some journalists may not be content to *report* the news, but instead work to *create* news through journalistic techniques designed to demean another's work or worth. We now live in a season in which some self-serving historians grovel for "truth" that would defame the dead and the defenseless. Some may be tempted to undermine what is sacred to others, or diminish the esteem of honored names, or demean the efforts of revered individuals. They seem to forget that the greatness of the very lives they examine is what endows the historian's work with any interest. But these temptations are not new. President Stephen L Richards expressed similar concern some thirty years ago:

"If a man of history has secured over the years a high place in the esteem of his countrymen and fellow men and has become imbedded in their affections, it has seemingly become a pleasing pastime for researchers and scholars to delve into the past of such a man, discover, if may be, some of his weaknesses and then write a book exposing hitherto unpublished alleged factual findings, all of which tends to rob the historic character of the idealistic esteem and veneration in which he may have been held through the years. . . .

"If an historic character has made a great contribution to country and society, and if his name and his deeds have been used over the generations to foster high ideals of character and service, what good is to be accomplished by digging out of the past and exploiting weaknesses, that perhaps a generous contemporary public forgave? . . .

"Perhaps, with propriety, we might look into . . . their objectives in destroying this idealism for our heroes and great men of history. Perhaps . . . their investigation and writing are prompted by a desire to show that men can be human, with human frailties, and still be great. If they were to say that that was their purpose, I would be inclined to doubt them, and much more inclined to believe that their writings were prompted by a desire to make money out of sensational, unsavory disclosures" (*Where Is Wisdom?* Salt Lake City: Deseret Book Co., 1955, 155).

Extortion by threat of disclosing truth is labeled "blackmail." Is sordid disclosure for personal attention or financial gain not closely related?

Paul perceived the wise judgment needed in wielding the powerful sword of truth as he taught: "Strive not about words to no profit, but to the subverting of the hearers.

"Study to shew thyself approved unto God, . . . *rightly dividing* the word of truth" (2 Timothy 2:14–15; emphasis added).

Rightly dividing the word of truth portends responsibility to communicate it accurately and without perversion, taking care not to injure or destroy. Hence so many scriptures caution the need to join truth with righteousness. Here are six examples:

"David my father . . . walked before thee in truth, and in righteousness" (1 Kings 3:6).

"Who shall dwell in thy holy hill?

"He that walketh uprightly, and worketh righteousness, and speaketh the truth in his heart.

"He that backbiteth not with his tongue, nor doeth evil to his neighbour, nor taketh up a reproach against his neighbour" (Psalm 15:1–3).

"Christ . . . is the word of truth and righteousness" (Alma 38:9).

"They did begin to keep his statutes and commandments, and to walk in truth and uprightness before him" (Helaman 6:34.)

"The fruit of the Spirit is in all goodness and righteousness and truth" (Ephesians 5:9).

"Let every man beware lest he do that which is not in truth and righteousness before me" (D&C 50:9).

Another pertains to the second coming of the Savior:

"Thus saith the Lord of hosts . . .

"They shall be my people, and I will be their

God, in truth and in righteousness" (Zechariah 8:7–8).

Don't misunderstand. I do *not* decry the revealing of negative information per se. A prosecutor who uncovers an embezzlement combines both truth and justice. A journalist who rightly reports betrayal of official trust combines truth with righteousness. Physicians who determined that old-fashioned "blood-letting" did more harm than good strengthened truth with light.

Too often, however, negative information is presented to further negative ends. In such cases, the facts are sometimes distorted, taken out of context, or at least badly understood.

Any who are tempted to rake through the annals of history, to use truth *unrighteously,* or to dig up "facts" with the intent to defame or destroy, should hearken to this warning of scripture:

"The righteousness of God [is] revealed from faith to faith: as it is written, The just shall live by faith.

"For the wrath of God is revealed from heaven against all ungodliness and unrighteousness of men, who hold the truth in unrighteousness" (Romans 1:17–18).

I repeat: "The wrath of God is . . . against all . . . who hold the truth in unrighteousness."

To anyone who, because of "truth," may be tempted to become a dissenter against the Lord and his anointed, weigh carefully your action in light of this sacred scripture:

"These dissenters, having the same instruction and the same information . . . yea, having been instructed in the same knowledge of the Lord, nevertheless, it is strange to relate, not long after their dessensions they became more hardened and impenitent, and . . . wicked . . . , entirely forgetting the Lord their God" (Alma 47:36).

When teachers and writers leave the lofty ethics of their honored professions, passing from legitimate reporting to feasting on sensational and pointless disclosures that appeal temporarily to a flattering few, their work slants more toward gossip than gospel. Even worse, if they "lift up [their] heel against mine anointed, saith the Lord, . . . their basket shall not be full, their houses and their barns shall perish, and they themselves shall be despised by those that flattered them" (D&C 121:16, 20).

Scriptures teach us that the pleasantries of prosperity, if tainted by seeds of selfishness and dissension against the Lord (or his anointed), comprise a dangerous combination. These verses are a solemn warning to us all:

"The very time when he doth prosper his people, yea, in the increase of their fields, their flocks and their herds, and in gold, and in silver, and in all manner of precious things . . . for the welfare and happiness of his people; yea, then is the time that they do harden their hearts, and do forget the Lord their God, and do trample under their feet the Holy One—yea, and this because of their ease, and their exceedingly great prosperity. . . .

"Yea, how quick to be lifted up in pride; yea, how quick to boast, and do all manner of that which is iniquity; and how slow are they to remember the Lord their God, and to give ear unto his counsels, yea, how slow to walk in wisdom's paths!

"Behold, they do not desire that the Lord their God, who hath created them, should rule and reign over them, notwithstanding his great goodness and his mercy towards them, they do set at naught his counsels, and they will not that he should be their guide" (Helaman 12:2–6).

In this country, academic freedom is something each of us prizes highly. Those in other

countries envy this opportunity enjoyed in our
great nation. It is a privilege that will be fostered
by keeping our university healthy, strong, and in
favor with God.

Each member of the Church bears the weight
of responsibility to consider the instrument of
truth *and more.* If truth is used by anyone in any
degree of unrighteousness, others, in the spirit
of *unity,* must act, bearing a responsibility *to turn*
and to help enlarge that person's perspective.

For if the true and righteous people are silent,
those who use truth in unrighteousness will pre-
vail. Speaking from his viewpoint in history,
Winston Churchill observed "how the malice of
the wicked was reinforced by the weakness of
the virtuous, . . . how the middle course adopted
from desires for safety and a quiet life may be
found to lead direct to the bull's-eye of disaster"
(*The Follies of the Victors,* 15–16).

We must realize that we are at war. The war

began before the world was and will continue. The forces of the adversary are extant upon the earth. All of our virtuous motives, if transmitted only by inertia and timidity, are no match for the resolute wickedness of those who oppose us.

Every individual associated with this Church should think, speak, and write throughout the world in consonance with the proverb:

"For my mouth shall speak truth; and wickedness is an abomination to my lips.

"All the words of my mouth are in righteousness; there is nothing . . . perverse in them" (Proverbs 8:7–8.)

The word *truth* is used 435 times in the scriptures. I have studied each of them. In 374 of those instances, truth is coupled in the same verse with some form of a strengthening term:

spirit	59
mercy(-iful)	47
right(-eousness)	42
holy(-iness)	36

judgment	23
light	23
grace	22
good(-ly, -liness)	21
love	18
peace	16
just(ice)	13
faith(-fulness)	12
loving kindness	11
wisdom	10
soberness	5
sanctified	4
kindness	3
sincerity	3
free	2
godliness	2
long-suffering	1
valiant	1
total	374

NOTE: In some verses, there is duplication of these listed terms.

The vast majority (374/435) of scriptural

references to this weighty word exemplify the importance of truth *and more.*

What do these figures tell us? Just as oxen may be equally yoked together to accomplish what one could not do alone, so the power of truth is augmented if equally yoked with righteousness or with mercy or with the spirit of love.

This concept extends beyond the walls of the university. It applies to our companions and children at home, where truth can even foment bitterness at times. Unless we couple truth with love and kindness, our focus may narrow to the tube of toothpaste squeezed at the top, the dust and cobwebs of work yet undone, the evidence of fingerprints on glass, or the hand-tools misplaced.

Truth, like justice, can be harsh and unforgiving when not tempered by mercy.

But when truth is magnified by mercy or

refined by righteousness, it can be converted from a force that can destroy to a force that can bless.

Ours is the glorious privilege of searching for truth, teaching the truth, and applying it righteously in service to others. We are sons and daughters of God engaged in his work.

As we embark on this great labor, I would invoke a blessing that success and joy may be ours. May we turn in unity toward the purpose that binds us all together—a commitment to truth *and more*—here, in our homes, and wherever we walk. May the deserved peace of heaven crown our efforts.

This is an edited version of a talk delivered at Brigham Young University on 27 August 1985 when Elder Nelson was serving as a member of the Quorum of the Twelve Apostles. The talk was published in the January 1986 edition of the *Ensign,* 69–73.